MW01206450

The Complete Guidebook to Exploiting Your RMR in Water Polo:

Learn How to Accelerate Your Resting Metabolic Rate to Drop Fat and Generate Lean Muscle

By

Joseph Correa

Certified Sports Nutritionist

COPYRIGHT

ACKNOWLEDGEMENTS

The realization and success of this book could not have been possible without the motivation and support of my family.

The Complete Guidebook to Exploiting Your RMR in Water Polo:

Learn How to Accelerate Your Resting Metabolic Rate to Drop Fat and Generate Lean Muscle

By

Joseph Correa

Certified Sports Nutritionist

CONTENTS

INTRODUCTION

The Complete Guidebook to Exploiting Your RMR in Water Polo by Joseph Correa

Nutrition is very important and what you eat will result in who you can potentially become. By adding lean muscle mass you automatically increase your RMR which can lead to improved performance with long lasting results.

If you want to make a serious change on your body and how it performs on a daily basis, you need to read this book and start applying it in your daily life.

By increasing your resting metabolic rate you will:

- Add more lean muscle mass.
- Reduce injuries and muscle cramps.
- Have more focus and are better able to stay concentrated for longer periods of time.
- Reduce fat at an accerated rate.
- Can outlast the competition.

HOW WILL THIS NUTRITION GUIDEBOOK BENEFIT ME?

Nutrition is very important and what you eat will result in who you can potentially become.

This nutrition book is the key to helping you achieve your goals. Joseph Correa, a certified sports nutritionist and a professional athlete who has dedicated himself to improving his performance through better nutrition and quality training exercises. Through his extensive knowledge and experience has created this easy to understand book on improved nutrition. He is convinced of the importance of proper nutrition and exercise to see long term results.

If you are looking to move on to the next level and are willing to make some sacrifices, then you have found the book that will solve to your nutritional needs by providing you with the necessary steps to a new beginning.

CHAPTER 1

The Complete Guidebook to Exploiting Your RMR in Water Polo

Learn How to Accelerate Your Resting Metabolic Rate to Drop Fat and Generate Lean Muscle

This nutrition guide serves as a perfect base for any athlete who wants to reach peak performance for the long term and be able to maintain it over the years. You will see long lasting results as an athlete primarily because of the focus on organic energy sources. This will allow you to perform at your very best for the longest period of time without any future negative effects on the brain and body unlike some enhanced performance substances that will strip the body of the essential elements to create natural processes in the body and alter them to create short term improvements.

All athletes should eat a lot of fruit, vegetables, and protein derived foods (chicken, eggs, turkey, fish, etc.). Complex carbohydrates intake should be cut down to a maximum of brown rice, pasta, all natural bread, and organic ingredients. In some places around the world where people have the longest life spans we can see several things in common: they drink mostly water, natural fruit juices, and milk. Everything they eat and drink is composed of natural, non-processed, non-canned, and non-preservative containing foods. By using this knowledge about people with longer life spans and their eating habits and other medical facts, I have created a nutrition guide that will help you to live and compete healthier and to live longer. It will also allow you to control your weight and the shape of your body better.

This book is divided into 3 water polo lifestyles:

Low Cardio Lifestyle Athlete (LCLA):

This dietary phase is for athletes who require less food containing complex carbohydrates (these include but are not limited to: pasta, brown rice, oatmeal, brown beans, lentils, etc.). These people do not need to store up that many energy reserves and therefore should have a higher percentage of foods containing proteins, legumes, vegetables, dairies fruits and other.

LCLA is for athletes who don't do more than 30 minutes of cardio per day as part of their training and also during competition. You can be flexible during competition since some conditions and environmental changes might change just how you can absorb food. This could be because of the country you are competing in, or you might feel nauseous before competing, or it can also be because of the food available in that area.

After the first month of completing this diet phase and complementing it in combination with your regular physical training regiment, you can decide to continue or adapt the diet to your needs in case you feel you need to add more protein or carbs or dairies.

Medium Cardio Lifestyle Athlete (MCLA):

This dietary phase is for athletes who require a specific percentage of foods containing complex carbohydrates (these include but are not limited to: pasta, brown rice, oatmeal, brown beans, lentils, etc.) to maintain a medium cardio-intensive lifestyle, while at the same time consuming a higher percentage of foods containing proteins, dairies, legumes, and fruits.

MCLA is for athletes who complete a minimum of 30 minutes of cardiovascular workouts as part of their daily physical training which may include (if you cross-train): swimming, walking, running, bicycling, jumping, rowing or playing sports that combine any of the aforementioned activities.

High Cardio Lifestyle Athlete (HCLA):

This dietary phase is for athletes who require a larger percentage of foods containing complex carbs to maintain their cardio intensive lifestyles in a balanced and healthy manner, while still maintaining a high percentage of foods containing protein, legumes, vegetables, fruits, and nuts.

HCLA is for people who train more than an hour of daily cardiovascular exercise. At least one hour of high intensity cardio workouts include (if you cross-train): running, swimming, rowing, jumping, or bicycling. This is especially important for athletes who do a lot of cardiovascular exercise as they require more carbohydrates to stay in good physical shape and to allow their bodies to recover.

The proper intake of proteins, fats and carbohydrates for non-athletes is:

Proteins 12%

Carbohydrates 58%

Fats 30%

The proper intake of proteins, fats and carbohydrates for athletes is:

Proteins 15-25%

Carbohydrates 50-65%

Fats 10-25%

Body builders eat more proteins to add muscle and bulk, with the proteins accounting for up to 35-40% of the diet for professional body builders.

Aerobic vs Anaerobic Physical Activity:

There are 2 main types of physical activity: Aerobic activity and anaerobic activity.

Anaerobic activity is defined as the activity undertaken without the presence of oxygen which cannot be sustained for long periods of time. This type of activity relies heavily on the fast twitch muscle fibers. Examples of anaerobic activity are weight lifting and sprinting. Such activities cannot be undertaken for long periods of time. This type of activity helps in building lean tissue and improves the body composition. The anaerobic capacity test is a test that measures the ability of the body to undertake exercise of a short duration and of a very high intensity. The Wingate cycle test is commonly used to test anaerobic capacity. Aerobic Fitness, also known as cardiovascular fitness is the ability of the body to perform an exercise over an extended period of time in the presence of oxygen. This type of activity relies heavily on slow twitch muscle fibers.

A training program which combines cardiovascular fitness and muscular fitness allows more oxygenated blood to be delivered per beat and increases the myoglobin in the muscles so that they can take up more amounts of oxygen, thus allowing more work to be done. This is why it is a smart decision to cross train. Being able to combine both aerobic with anaerobic training will give you the best results before, during, and after competition.

HELPFUL TIPS:

➢ Keep any condiments in your food to a minimum of one teaspoon per meal. Just enough to give your food some flavor.

➢ Instead of sugar, use honey to sweeten your drinks and food. If you absolutely have to use sugar make sure it's brown sugar.

Sports nutrition is more than just what you eat;

It's when and how you eat!

Drink at least 6-8 glasses of water per day

Drink 1 glass of water when you wake up, 1 before every meal, and 1 before going to sleep.

Eat 6 small to medium size meals per day

You should be eating every three hours. Use a timer, a stop watch or your cell phone to keep track of time as this is just as important as what you eat. If you eat small to medium size meals every three hours, you allow your body to digest food in an efficient manner and in a way that does not overwork the digestive system. Some people eat three large meals a day and then have to wait several hours until they don't feel full again but this is exactly what not to do.

Nutritional Guide for L C L A's

Monday – Saturday (daily percentage to be consumed)

20% complex carbs – 20% proteins – 30% vegetables and legumes – 15% fruits and nuts – 15% dairy foods and snacks

Or the equivalent in daily servings

Carbs (1-2 servings) – proteins (3-4 servings) – vegetables and legumes (3-6 servings) – Fruits and nuts (1.5-3 servings) – dairy foods and snacks (1.5 servings)

Sunday

(Some athletes don't train on Sundays or once a week so one day per week the food servings will change. We are using Sunday as that day.)

15% carbs – 25% proteins – 20% vegetables and legumes – 20% fruits and nuts – 20% dairy foods and snacks

Or the equivalent in servings

Carbs (1.5-3 servings) – proteins (2.5-3 servings) – vegetables and legumes (2 Servings) – Fruits and nuts (2-3 servings) – dairy foods and Snacks (2 servings)

*The percentages shown are for the daily consumption of these food groups and the servings are for the maximum amount of times you are allowed to consume these food groups. Follow the food group charts provided at the beginning of the book as a guide to what you can eat except for the dairies which you are free to choose the type and amount due to the variety of preferences and medical conditions out there.

Nutritional Guide for M C L A's

Monday - Saturday

15% carbs – 30% proteins – 25% vegetables and legumes – 15% fruits and nuts – 15% dairy foods and snacks

Or the equivalent in daily servings

Carbs (1.5-3 servings) – proteins (3-6 servings) – vegetables and legumes (2.5-6 servings) – Fruits and nuts (1.5-3 servings) – dairy foods and snacks (1.5-3 servings)

Sunday

(Some athletes don't train on Sundays or once a week so one day per week the food servings will change. We are using Sunday as that day.)

25% carbs – 20 % proteins – 20% vegetables and legumes – 20% fruits and nuts – 15% dairy foods and snacks

Or the equivalent in servings

Carbs (2.5-3 servings) – proteins (2-5 servings) – vegetables and legumes (2 servings) – Fruits and nuts (2 servings) – dairy foods and snacks (1.5 servings)

The percentages shown are for the daily consumption of these food groups and the servings are for the maximum amount of times you are allowed to consume these food groups. Follow the food group charts provided at the beginning of the book as a guide to what you can eat except for the dairies which you are free to choose the type and amount due to the variety of preferences and medical conditions out there.

Nutritional Guide for H C L A's

Monday - Saturday

20% carbs – 25% proteins – 20% vegetables and legumes – 15% fruits and nuts – 20% dairy foods and snacks

Or the equivalent in daily servings

Carbs (2 servings) – proteins (2.5 servings) – vegetables and legumes (2 servings) – Fruits and nuts (1.5 servings) – dairy foods and snacks (2 servings)

Sunday

(Some athletes don't train on Sundays or once a week so one day per week the food servings will change. We are using Sunday as that day.)

25% carbs – 20% proteins – 15% vegetables and legumes – 20% fruits and nuts – 20% dairy foods and snacks

Or the equivalent in servings

Carbs (2.5 servings) – proteins (2 servings) – vegetables and legumes (1.5 servings) – Fruits and nuts (2 servings) – dairy foods and snacks (2 servings)

*The percentages shown are for the daily consumption of these food groups and the servings are for the maximum amount of times you are allowed to consume these food groups. Follow the food group charts provided at the beginning of the book as a guide to what you can eat except for the dairies which you are free to choose the type and amount due to the variety of preferences and medical conditions out there.

CHAPTER 2

THE FASTEST PATH TO A LEANER BODY

RMR: Become a Calorie Burning Machine

RMR is also known as resting metabolic rate and is the number of calories burned while your body is at rest because of normal body functions such as the heart rate and the breathing function. **This accounts for 75% of the total calories burned during the day.** This can vary from one person to another depending on age, amount of fat in your body, and other factors. The less fat you have in your body and the more muscle you have the higher the RMR will be and the faster you will burn calories at rest, even in your sleep. This is what some people consider as having a good metabolism but it really equates to having a high RMR. Having a high RMR will make you leaner and make easier for you to stay leaner every day. How to do you accomplish this? You can do this by changing what you eat to reduce fats and sugars, and by adding muscle to your body.

Each and every day is an opportunity to get back in shape. When you're tired of work and constantly busy with all the tedious things in life, you stop thinking about the importance of taking care of your body and mind. For this reason, I have prepared a daily schedule to help you <u>get in shape all day even while you eat, sleep, and breathe.</u> How is this possible? You can do this by simply by accelerating your metabolism. A natural way of doing this is by making small changes in your life that have an immediate effect on your body.

This daily schedule can be changed to accommodate your lifestyle as well as your training schedule. <u>Things you already do on a normal day will be highlighted in bold just to remind you that you're not really changing your day to day schedule at all.</u>

Remember, you are the only one that can keep yourself motivated enough to go through with the schedule. Working out every day and sticking to this nutrition guide requires sacrifice and being able to let go of temptations.

Improving your breathing techniques

Static breathing exercises, Yoga, Pilates, stretching, and other forms of breathing exercises will help you reduce your stress levels.

Less stress = A longer life

These exercises are for both men and women. They have changed my life and I am sure they will do the same for you. These are just some of the benefits you will see:

- Increased flexibility
- Stronger back and core muscles
- Improved posture
- Reduced stress

The Ideal Nutrition and Workout Schedule

Monday - Friday

7:00 AM   Drink one glass of water when you *wake up*.

7:15 AM   Complete a minimum of 5 abdominal exercises or 5 stretching exercises.

8:00 AM   Drink a glass of water, milk, or juice and then *eat breakfast*. Base your breakfast on the diet plan explained in chapter 1.

8:30 AM   Train as you normally would on a weekday.

10:00 AM   Drink one glass of water.

11:00 AM   Eat a fruit along with a multigrain bar (or another snack based on the list provided in chapter 1.). You can add or replace it with a yogurt or slices of a protein (turkey, ham, roast beef, fish, poultry, etc.).

11:10 AM	After having your snack make sure to take a 5 minute break to stretch and breathe, or simply relax your body so that you prepare your body for lunch in a peaceful environment.
2:00 PM	Drink a glass of water, juice, milk or other liquid and then *have lunch*.
2:45 PM	Rest at least 30 minutes to 1 hour to allow your body to fully digest the food.
4:00 PM	Start your afternoon training which might include going to

the gym or simply resting if your morning training was enough.

5:00 PM   Complete abdominal exercises.

6:30 PM   Drink a glass of water, milk, or juice before *having dinner*. Remember to eat only foods explained in the nutrition plan in the first chapter.

8:30 PM   Eat a snack if your still hungry. Make sure to eat small quantities. <u>Remember that after dark you do not eat any carbs, fruits or foods that contain either one.</u>

10:00 PM   You should drink at least one glass of water before going to *sleep even if you sleep earlier or later than the time provided.*

Note:

You can adjust the schedule and the exercises as long as all the steps are completed and are in order. Also, make sure you stay within the 3 hour time difference between meals and drink a minimum of 6 – 8 glasses of water before the end of the day.

Improving the quality of events in your life and daily schedule will help you lose weight even while you are sleeping as your metabolism will accelerate at a faster rate and will move its way to your sleeping hours.

Saturday

For Saturday's schedule we are simply going to replace the time at work with time at home, entertainment, or doing some chores. Saturday would look something like this:

7:00 AM   Drink one glass of water when you *wake up*.

7:15 AM   Do a 5 minute morning stretch to get your muscles relaxed and ready for the day ahead.

8:00 AM   Drink a glass of water, milk, or juice and then *eat breakfast*. Base your breakfast on the diet plan explained in chapter 1.

8:30 AM   Train as you normally would on a weekday.

10:00 AM   Drink one glass of water.

11:00 AM	Eat a fruit along with a multigrain bar (or another snack based on the list provided in chapter 1.). You can add or replace it with a yogurt or slices of a protein (turkey, ham, roast beef, fish, poultry, etc.).
11:10 AM	After having your snack make sure to take a 5 minute break to stretch and breathe, or simply relax your body so that you prepare your body for lunch in a peaceful environment.
2:00 PM	Drink a glass of water, juice, milk or other liquid and then *have lunch*.
2:45 PM	Rest
5:30 PM	Drink a glass of water, milk, or juice before *having dinner*. Remember to eat only foods in

the nutrition guide provided at the beginning of this book.

8:30 PM   Eat a small meal and include a glass of water with this meal.

10:00 PM   Drink a glass of water before going to *sleep*.

CHAPTER 3

JUMP-STARTING YOUR METABOLISM

Enhancing Your Performance through a

More Efficient Body

What you do if I told you that you could get in shape 24 hours a day? Sound impossible? Let me tell you how to do it through a very simple process that might surprise you in a sense because of its simplicity but first we will focus on the three main components of staying in shape and losing weight. They are: Patience, repetition, and focus.

Patience

It takes time to gain weight. Some people spend a year or more increasing their weight without ever controlling it. Dropping all that weight that has taken so long to accumulate takes time if you want lasting results. Let me repeat that one more time because it's a difficult concept to understand. It takes time to drop all the weight you have accumulated over the years. If you want quick results just work smarter and improve your nutrition. If you lose weight fast, be sure that it will come back just as fast if you don't continue to do what you did to drop it. *Don't fall for the easy way out* because it won't last and you'll be right back where you started. Be patient as small decreases in weight are more valuable in the long run than large ones that come right back. Your body will gradually adjust to the exercise routines and the nutritional plan. That means you will be building off your new results each time. Just be patient.

Over time your body weight works like a seesaw.

Your weight will increase as time goes by if you don't take the necessary steps to maintain it at a healthy level and it will decrease as time goes by if you work hard to control it. Maintaining your body weight is a matter of balance between nutrition and exercise.

Repetition

Changing your lifestyle takes time and it takes permanent decisions. If you decide to start working out but find yourself training once a week or every other week, then you obviously know what type of results you will have. You've got to be consistent. Also, you need to be repetitive in what you, from the first day of the month until the last day of the month. It sounds like a lot of work, but you have to realize that you already do a lot of things in a consistent manner that you might not have noticed. Do you eat at least three times a day, every day of every month of the year? <u>Do you watch TV at least an hour every day of every month?</u> Do you change your clothes every day of every month of the year? And do you take a shower every day of every month of the year? If you answered "yes" to these questions, it means you do a lot of things in a consistent way. I bet a lot of people never even realize they do all these things every day. It's definitely something you should use to your advantage, by simply adding some exercises and an effective diet plan to these everyday activities.

There are "quick fixes" that can get you where you want to be but most of the time they'll have some sort of side effect or health risk involved. That's not what this book is about. You're working on obtaining <u>long term results that will last</u> and that will eventually become a part of your life. That's why it's important to stick to these exercises and allow them to become a part of your daily life.

The most important thing is to be consistent if you want long term results so stay focused on getting there.

Focus

Focus is the art of being able to concentrate on something for a determined period of time. That's what I want you to do with your new exercise routine and dietary plan. Stay focused no matter what. Stay focused on the objective at hand. Stay focused on your new lifestyle. Work at it every day because it's your life and it's up to you and no one else to make it better.

HOW TO JUMP-START YOUR METABOLISM

We spoke about increasing your RMR in the last chapter but now let's go into more detail.

Step 1: Start doing more exercise, preferably the exercises that involve increasing the amount of muscle in your body. Your body will to have to regenerate muscle tissue during the night time and this will contribute towards burning more energy. By doing this, you will lose weight and get fitter during the entire day!

Step 2: Follow the nutritional instructions described in chapter 1. Eating better and at scheduled times will change the short and long term effects your body and mind will have over time by reducing fat and simple sugar intake. This will help you to have a better defense mechanism that in turn will prevent you from getting sick or injured. It will boost your energy levels as well as help prevent future health problems such as obesity and heart disease. This is just to name a few of the most common ailments affecting our society today.

Step 3: Non-athletes need to drink a minimum of 6 to 8 glasses of water during the day, <u>especially one glass upon waking up and one before going to sleep.</u> As an athlete you should drink 6-10 glasses of water.

The Right Way to Drink Water

Water intake before the exercise, during the exercise and after the exercise should be properly planned.

A) Before training or competition consume 14-18 ounces of water two hours before any exercise. The two hour gap is enough to fully hydrate the body and leave enough time for excess water to come out of the system.

Take 5-7 ounces of water just 15 minutes before training.

B) During training or competition an athlete must constantly keep hydrating the body every 20-25 minutes with 5-10 ounces of water. Sports drinks are good sources of sodium which needs to be replenished in competition but should be mixed with some water to dilute the high sugar content they usually have to make them taste good.

Athletes who perspire excessively should consume 1.5 g of sodium and 2.3 g of chloride each day (or 3.8 g of salt) to replace the amount lost through perspiration. The maximum amount should not exceed 5.8 g of salt each day (2.3 g of sodium). Consult with your doctor if you have any of these medical conditions: elevated blood pressure, coronary heart disease, diabetes, and kidney disease, etc. These athletes should avoid consuming salt at the upper level. Endurance athletes and other individuals who are involved in strenuous activities are allowed to consume more sodium to offset sweat losses. The carbonates in the sports drinks also help the muscles perform better. Athletes should also have an adequate intake of 4.7 g of potassium per day to blunt the effects of salt, lower blood pressure, and reduce the risk of kidney stones and bone loss. Athletes should also eat foods rich in potassium such as bananas and prunes.

C) After training or competition an athlete should replace all lost fluids by drinking approximately 20 ounces of fluid for every pound of weight lost.

Step 4: Sleep at least 5 hours but no more than 10 per day and take power naps during the day if you feel you need to get more rest. Sleeping allows your body to recover from the wear and tear you experience every day. It's also a good time for your body to recover so that you can continue training the following day. Sleeping is an excellent way to relieve your body and mind of any excess stress that has accumulated during the day. Sleeping is important so make sure you get adequate hours of sleep every night.

Step 5: Working your cardiovascular endurance is a great way to accelerate your metabolism which will also strengthen your heart. Make sure you do as much aerobic exercise as possible without getting injured. Besides static exercises and stretching, aerobic exercises will provide you with one of the most important tools you can have towards having a higher resting metabolic rate which we talked about in the last chapter. Some good aerobic exercises you can do to cross train are: running, swimming, jumping, roller-blading, skiing, rowing, karate, and playing sports that require any combination of these. A good cardiovascular exercise you can do after lunch is walk up and down stairs at a slow pace and at a low intensity level. If you work or live in a building that has stairs, make sure you take advantage of this. A building with two floors would be sufficient since you can go up and down the same steps. Make sure you do this for at least 5 minutes to make it worthwhile. After eating, always try to do some form of low-intensity aerobic exercise besides walking up and down stairs. This might be one of the most important changes you make towards improving your overall health and fitness.

Our goal in this chapter is to naturally accelerate your metabolism by staying as active as possible during most of the day which will increase your RMR. A faster metabolism helps your body stay lean and fit but you want to make sure you do this naturally (without the use of artificial substances) and gradually so that these changes are easily maintained in months and years to come.

CHAPTER 4

SUPERIOR WATER POLO PERFORMANCE THROUGH ANTIOXIDANTS

Faster Recovery for Faster Results

A number of elements in our body such as sunlight and pollution in our environment produce oxidation leading to the production of dangerous chemical compounds called free radicals. Free radicals can lead to serious cellular damage, which is the common pathway for cancer, ageing, and a variety of other diseases. Free radicals are highly reactive and pose a major threat by reacting with cell membranes in chain reactions leading to the death of the cells. Antioxidants are molecules that can help in destroying the free radicals so that the body can be free from the dangers associated with the free radicals. Moreover, athletes should have a keen interest in them because of health concerns and the prospect of enhanced performance and/or recovery after exercise. The way antioxidants work is that they can react with the free radicals and shut down the chain reaction leading to the death of the DNA cells and thus save them.

The main sources of antioxidants are:

1. Vitamin E: It is an antioxidant and helps protect cells from damage. It is also important for the health of red blood cells. Vitamin E is found in many foods such as vegetable oils, nuts, and leafy green vegetables. Avocados, wheat germ, and whole grains are also good sources of this vitamin.

2. Beta-carotene: It is a precursor to vitamin A (retinol) and is present in liver, egg yolk, milk, butter, spinach, carrots, tomatoes, and grains.

3. Vitamin C: It is needed to form collagen, a tissue that helps in holding cells together. It is essential for healthy bones, teeth, gums, and blood vessels. It helps the body absorb iron and calcium, aids in wound healing, and contributes to brain function. You will find high levels of vitamin C in red berries, kiwifruit, red and green bell peppers, tomatoes, broccoli, spinach, and juices made from guava, grapefruit, and orange.

4. Selenium: It is a trace element and is also an important antioxidant.

Some Popular Antioxidants are Mentioned Below:

Strengthening our immune system will help you absorb antioxidants and protect you from free radicals which can be done through exercise. That's why a combination of cardiovascular and weight training in combination with added antioxidants in your diet will improve you performance and allow you to have less low energy or sick days. By consuming more antioxidants your recovery phase will be faster which will allow you to compete sooner than normal.

Project the Right Image through a

Better Posture to Win More

Studies have shown that athletes who project a strong positive image are prone to being more successful and have a stronger immune system. Having a strong immune system will keep you healthier and prone to less injuries which equates to having the prospect of winning more simply because you can compete more often.

Definitive change from the caveman era to now is our posture. For some reason a lot of athletes look like they are back in the caveman era. Maybe some athletes have this hunched posture because they don't work on flexibility and back strengthening exercises or maybe because of lack of confidence. Whatever may be the reason, an athlete's posture says a lot about how they feel and what they project specially to their competition. Showing a lack of confidence to your competition will only motivate them to do better. To succeed more as an athlete start showing more confidence through a better posture even when you are not competing.

Most of us forget that as we get older our backs hunch even more and it becomes more difficult to stay straight. I would rather work on having a better posture now than later because later might never come. I forgot to mention that not standing up straight makes you look fatter as well. So if you want to start looking thinner, start standing up straight! For this and many other reasons, it's essential to focus on your posture.

It has often been overlooked by many but can help you get to a better figure faster than you can imagine. Did you know that by walking in a slouched position you are actually making your stomach muscles lazier and thus promoting that shape of abdominal muscles? Not a good habit to have. By walking straight you are actually working your abs.

Posture is a matter of habit

You must concentrate on maintaining a straight posture all the time. Focus on keeping a good posture when you walk, when you sit and when you stand. Posture is also very important when you eat because it helps food pass through your digestive system easier than if you were slouched. Chewing your food better can contribute to the reduction or better yet, prevention, of digestion or acid reflux related issues.

Also, *consider that no matter how hard you work and how good a body you may have, if you slouch, you just ruined the picture (the image of yourself and what you project to others) and made all that effort become almost unnoticed.* For this specific reason, I want to remind you how vital it is to concentrate, work on and make a habit of standing, sitting and walking with a straight posture.

Key points to having a better posture are:

1. Your Shoulders should be relaxed and below your neck height.
2. Your Chest should be out and shoulders back.
3. Your Head needs to be perpendicular to the ground. (Imagine drawing a straight line from your chin to the ground.)
4. Your Eyes should be focused on the horizon NOT on the ground.

CHAPTER 5

INCREASE YOUR PROTEIN WITH HOMEMADE PROTEIN BAR RECIPES FOR WATER POLO

Pushing Your Body to the Next Stage in Muscle Growth

Preparing is half the battle. Start by buying some of the ingredients in the recipes you like the most from the ones provided below. Make sure you choose ingredients to consume immediately and others that won't perish as fast so that you can plan on making some protein bars to eat now while other protein bars for another day.

PROTEIN BAR RECIPES FOR WATER POLO

1. Vanilla pudding bars

Ingredients:

1.5 scoops of protein powder (vanilla)

1 cup of oat flakes

1 package of pudding (vanilla flavor)

2 cups of skimmed milk

Preparation:

Mix the ingredients until you get a sticky mass. It should take about few minutes. Cook briefly, about 3-4 minutes, on a low temperature. Pour the mixture into a glass or a metal protein bar containers. You should get 8 protein bars with this mixture. Refrigerate overnight.

Nutritional values:

Carbohydrates 35g

Sugar 6.74g

Protein 52g

Total fat (good monounsaturated fat) 1,38g

Sodium 376mg

Potassium 880mg

Calcium 684.7mg

Iron 1.31mg

Vitamins (Vitamin C; B-6; B-12; A-RAE; A-IU; E; D; D-D2+D3; K; Thianin; Riboflavin; Niacin)

Calories 257

2. Low-fat yogurt bars

Ingredients:

½ cup of low fat fresh cheese

2 cups of low-fat yogurt

4 scoops of whey protein (vanilla)

½ cups of oat flakes

Preparation:

Mix the ingredients in a blender. Put it in a freezer for about an hour. Cut into 8 protein bars and keep in a refrigerator. Your protein bars are ready to eat after 2-3 hours.

Nutritional values:

Carbohydrates 19g

Sugar 5,76g

Protein 27,5g

Total fat 3.3g

Sodium 268,7mg

Potassium 535,3mg

Calcium 456,6mg

Iron 0,73mg

Vitamins (Vitamin C total ascorbic acid; B-6; B-12;
A-RAE; A-IU; E; D; D-D2+D3; K-phylloquinone;
Thianin; Riboflavin; Niacin)

Calories 228

3. Cottage cheese bars

Ingredients:

1 cup of low fat creamy cottage cheese

4 scoops of protein powder (chocolate)

1 cup of barley flakes cereal

2 tbsp of honey

½ tsp of cinnamon

Preparation:

Put the cheese with protein powder, honey and cinnamon in a large bowl. Mix the ingredients with an electric mixer. Mix until you get a smooth mixture. Add the barley flakes and mix few more minutes. If your mixture is too thick, add a little water. Pour the mixture into previously greased pan and refrigerate for about an hour. Cut into 10 protein bars. They are now ready to eat.

Nutritional values:

Carbohydrates 21g

Sugar 8.58g

Protein 24g

Total fat 4g

Sodium 221,2mg

Potassium 361,1mg

Calcium 333.5mg

Iron 5.23mg

Vitamins (Vitamin C total ascorbic acid; B-6; B-12; Folate-DFE; A-RAE; A-IU; E-alpha-tocopherol; D; D-D2+D3; K-phylloquinone; Thianin; Riboflavin; Niacin)

Calories 190

4. Protein bars of coconut and vanilla

Ingredients:

1 scoop of vanilla protein powder

1/4 cup coconut flakes

1/4 cup chopped coconut

1/4 cup milk (skimmed)

3 tbsp of melted dark chocolate (85% of cocoa)

Preparation:

Soak the coconut peaces into water and let it stand for about an hour. Meanwhile, mix the vanilla protein powder and coconut flakes with milk. You have to use skimmed milk. This significantly influences the nutritional value of your protein bars. The electric mixer will do the job. Now add chopped coconut peaces and mix well. Pour the mixture into a small pan and sprinkle with melted chocolate. Let it stand in the refrigerator for few hours. Cut into 3 large protein bars.

Nutritional values:

Carbohydrates 20g

Sugar 9.53g

Protein 19.25g

Total fat 6.06g

Sodium 53mg

Potassium 353mg

Calcium 302mg

Iron 12,6

Vitamins (Vitamin C total ascorbic acid; B-6; B-12; Folate-DFE; A-RAE; A-IU; E-alpha-tocopherol; D; D-D2+D3; K-phylloquinone; Thianin; Riboflavin; Niacin)

Calories 256

5. Protein bars with orange and goji berries

Ingredients:

1 scoop of organic protein powder (tasteless)

3/4 cup of ground almonds

1/4 cup of grated coconut

3/4 cup of goji berries

1 cup of coconut milk

½ glass of water

1 tsp of vanilla extract

1 tsp of grated orange peel

1 tsp of chili powder

3 tbsp of grated dark chocolate with 85% of cocoa

Preparation:

This recipe will give you 5 super healthy protein bars. First you need to mix the grated orange peel with chili, vanilla extract and coconut milk. Cook on a low temperature for 10-15 minutes. Allow it to cool. Meanwhile, mix the protein powder, almonds, grated coconut, goji berries and water in a blender for few minutes. Add the cooled mixture of chili, vanilla extract, orange peel and coconut milk and mix for another 1-2 minutes. Pour the mixture into 8 protein bar containers and sprinkle with dark chocolate on top. Refrigerate.

Nutritional values:

Carbohydrates 14.5g

Sugar 2.61g

Protein 13.5g

Total fat 16.6 g

Sodium 49,5mg

Potassium 331mg

Calcium 121,8mg

Iron 37.6mg

Vitamins (Vitamin C; B-6; B-12; A-RAE; D; D-D2+D3; K-phylloquinone; Thianin; Riboflavin; Niacin)

Calories 248.8 kcal

6. Protein bars with pumpkin seeds

Ingredients:

2 small cooked carrots

1/2 cup of protein powder - vanilla

1/4 cup of minced pumpkin seeds

1/4 cup of skimmed milk

1 tsp of pumpkin seeds butter

2 tbsp of brown sugar

¼ cup of water

Preparation:

Wash and peel the carrots. Cut into smaller pieces and let it boil for about 20 minutes (until they are completely cooked). Allow it to cool. Melt the pumpkin seeds butter and add sugar. Mix well for few seconds. Then add milk and protein powder. Cook this mixture for few minutes (3-4 minutes) and add carrots. Mash until smooth, adding water constantly. Divide the mixture into 4 medium containers and sprinkle with minced pumpkin seeds. Let it stand in refrigerator for few hours.

Nutritional values:

Carbohydrates 21g

Sugar 7,93g

Protein 17.5

Total fat 9.3g

Sodium 52,3mg

Potassium 289mg

Calcium 127,6mg

Iron 12,3mg

Vitamins (Vitamin C total ascorbic acid; B-6; B-12; Folate-DFE; A-RAE; A-IU; E-alpha-tocopherol; D; D-D2+D3; K-phylloquinone; Thianin)

Calories 200

7. Orange juice protein bars

Ingredients:

3½ cups of oatmeal

1½ cups of milk powder (1.5% fat)

4 tbsp of protein powder (any flavor you like)

1 cup of honey

2 beaten egg whites

1 cup of orange juice

1 tsp of cinnamon

Preparation:

Sprinkle a baking pan with some low fat baking spray. Mix oatmeal, powdered milk and protein powder in a bowl. In a separate bowl, combine egg whites, orange juice and honey. Stir the liquid mixture into the dry. The mixture should be thick and similar to cookies dough. Pour the mixture into the baking pan and bake in preheated oven, at 350 degrees for 10-15 minutes. The edges should be crispy and brown. Cut into 10 pieces and allow it to cool. Leave in a refrigerator overnight

Nutritional values:

Carbohydrates 18.7g

Sugar 3.2g

Protein 17.5g

Total fat 14.8 g

Sodium 51,5mg

Potassium 328mg

Calcium 126,8mg

Iron 29.2mg

Vitamins (Vitamin C; B-6; B-12; A-RAE; D; D-D2+D3; K-phylloquinone; Thianin; Riboflavin; Niacin)

Calories 248.8 kcal

8. Coconut protein bars

Ingredients:

1 tip full scoop of vanilla protein powder

2 tip full scoops of coconut flour

½ cup of milk

2 large cubes of dark chocolate (80% of cocoa)

Preparation:

This is super easy recipe and it should take no more than 10 minutes. You will have very tasty protein bars. Mix the protein powder with coconut flour and pour milk. You should get a compact mixture. If it's too thick for your taste, add some water. You can't go wrong with this recipe. If you overdo with liquid, add dry ingredients, and vice versa. When you're finished, make 3 protein bars with this mixture and leave them in the refrigerator to squeeze slightly. Meanwhile, prepare the chocolate coating by melting the chocolate on a low temperature. Spread the chocolate over the protein bars and leave in the refrigerator for few hours.

Nutritional values:

Carbohydrates 14.5g

Sugar 2.61g

Protein 13.5g

Total fat 16.6 g

Sodium 49,5mg

Potassium 331mg

Calcium 121,8mg

Iron 37.6mg

Vitamins (Vitamin C total ascorbic acid; B-6; B-12; A-RAE; A-IU; E; D; D-D2+D3; K-phylloquinone; Thianin; Riboflavin; Niacin)

Calories 176.8 kcal

9. Almond protein bars

Ingredients:

¼ cup of grated almonds,

¼ cup of skimmed almond milk

¼ cup of freshly ground flax seeds

½ cup of coconut flower

3 egg whites

½ tsp of salt

¼ cup of almond butter

1 tbsp of honey

organic vanilla extract

½ cup of raisins

Preparation:

Mix the almonds, flax seeds, coconut flower, salt and egg whites in a food processor. Melt the almond butter until nice golden color and add honey, milk and vanilla extract. Let it cook for few minutes. Add the mixture of almonds, flax seeds, coconut flower, salt and eggs and let it boil. Then add the raisins. Let it cool in a freezer for about an hour. Cut into 8 protein bars and leave in the refrigerator overnight.

Nutritional values:

Carbohydrates 21.8g

Sugar 8.61g

Protein 18.3g

Total fat 14.6 g

Sodium 54,5mg

Potassium 327mg

Calcium 112,8mg

Iron 25.3mg

Vitamins (Vitamin C; B-6; B-12; A-RAE; D; D-D2+D3; K-phylloquinone; Thianin; Riboflavin; Niacin)

Calories 232.7 kcal

10.Chocolate muesli protein bars

Ingredients:

3 cups of oatmeal

1 cup of chocolate muesli

½ cup of grated almonds

½ cup of grated hazelnuts

one cup of prunes, cut into small pieces (raisins, figs or Optional),

½ cup of peanuts,

2 tbsp of cocoa powder

4 scoops of chocolate protein powder

2 glasses of skimmed milk

Preparation:

Mix the ingredients in a large bowl until the mixture hardens. You can use an electric mixer for this. Pour the mixture into a baking pan and bake for about 30 minutes in preheated oven (350 degrees). It should get a nice golden brown color.

Then remove it from the oven and cut into 8 protein bars. Let it stand for few hours. Your protein bars are ready to eat.

Nutritional values:

Carbohydrates 21.3g

Sugar 8.2g

Protein 19.4g

Total fat 13.4g

Sodium 52mg

Potassium 345mg

Calcium 133,2mg

Iron 23.6mg

Vitamins (Vitamin C; B-6; B-12; A-RAE; D; D-D2+D3; K-phylloquinone; Thianin; Riboflavin; Niacin)

Calories 239 kcal

11. Cranberries protein bars

Ingredients:

3 cups of oatmeal

½ cup of almonds

1 cup of dried cranberries

4 tbsp of peanut butter

1 glass of skimmed milk

4 scoops of vanilla protein powder

Preparation:

Mix the oatmeal, almonds and cranberries in a bowl. Melt the peanut butter on a low temperature. You want to add some milk before it melts – this way the peanut butter won't burn. When the peanut butter melts, add vanilla protein powder and let it boil. Remove from heat and allow it to cool. Now add the dry mixture and stir well. Pour the mixture into 5 protein bar containers and leave in the refrigerator. After about 4 hours, your protein bars are finished and ready to eat.

Nutritional values:

Carbohydrates 19.6g

Sugar 7.9g

Protein 19.3g

Total fat 12.3 g

Sodium 51,5mg

Potassium 298mg

Calcium 147mg

Iron 23.6mg

Vitamins (Vitamin C; B-6; B-12; A-RAE; D; D-D2+D3; K-phylloquinone; Thianin; Riboflavin; Niacin)

Calories 224 kcal

12.Protein bars with coconut and lemon

Ingredients:

1 cup of chopped almonds or almond slices

1.5 cups of raisins

1 cup unsweetened coconut milk

1 tbsp of lemon zest

2 tbsp of lemon juice

Preparation:

Put all the ingredients into a blender. You want to soak the raisins in water for five minutes before you put them in a blender. Fill 5 protein bar containers with this mixture and leave in a freezer for about an hour. And that's it! Your protein bars are ready.

Nutritional values:

Carbohydrates 14.3g

Sugar 2,9g

Protein 14.9g

Total fat 13g

Sodium 29mg

Potassium 361mg

Calcium 112mg

Iron 13.6mg

Vitamins (Vitamin C; B-6; B-12; A-RAE; D; D-D2+D3; K-phylloquinone; Thianin; Riboflavin; Niacin)

Calories 200 kcal

13.Simple protein bars

Ingredients:

2 scoops of Whey protein powder

1 cup of organic oatmeal

1 glass of skimmed milk

4 tbsp of peanut butter

4 tbsp of honey

1 tbsp of cocoa powder

½ cup of freshly crushed flaxseed

Preparation:

Bind the Whey protein powder and cocoa powder with milk. Add honey and oatmeal. You want to stir well to get a dough-like mixture. Melt the peanut butter in a frying pan and fry crushed flax seeds for about 5 minutes. Remove from pan and add to the mixture. Pour the dough like mixture into the baking pan and sprinkle with flax seeds. Bake at 350 degrees, in preheated oven, for 10 minutes. Allow it to cool for a while and cut into 4 protein bars. Leave in the refrigerator overnight.

Nutritional values:

Carbohydrates 19g

Sugar 4.6g

Protein 18.5g

Total fat 12.2 g

Sodium 52mg

Potassium 401mg

Calcium 117mg

Iron 19.6mg

Vitamins (Vitamin C; B-6; B-12; A-RAE; D; D-D2+D3; K-phylloquinone; Thianin; Riboflavin; Niacin)

Calories 224 kcal

14.Almond butter protein bars

Ingredients:

1 cup of almond butter

3 tbsp of vanilla protein powder

½ cup of maple syrup

2 egg whites

2 cups of oatmeal

½ cup of grated coconut

1 tsp of baking powder

Preparation:

Use electric mixer to mix almond butter, protein powder and maple syrup. Add egg whites. Stir in the oatmeal, coconut and baking powder. Make a dough with this mixture. Pour it into a baking pan and bake in a preheated oven for about 10 minutes. It should have a nice light brown color. Allow it to cool well and cut into 4 protein bars. Keep them in a sealed bowl.

Nutritional values:

Carbohydrates 19g

Sugar 5.2g

Protein 17.3g

Total fat 12g

Sodium 51.1mg

Potassium 212mg

Calcium 114mg

Iron 22mg

Vitamins (Vitamin C; B-6; B-12; A-RAE; D; D-D2+D3; K-phylloquinone; Thianin; Riboflavin; Niacin)

Calories 217 kcal

15.Muesli chocolate bars

Ingredients:

1.5 cups quinoa flakes

½ cup of chopped walnuts

¼ cup of unsweetened, shredded coconut

¼ cup of sweetened vanilla protein powder

1 egg

2/3 cup of Greek yogurt

1/3 cup unsweetened almond butter

3 tbsp of honey

2 tbsp of melted coconut oil

1 tbsp of lemon peel

½ cup of raisins

Preparation:

Preheat oven to 350 degrees. Grease the baking pan with coconut oil. Spread evenly quinoa flakes, chopped walnuts and shredded coconut and bake for about 6-8 minutes. Meanwhile, mix the Greek yogurt with egg, melted almond butter, honey, lemon peel and raisins. Remove the nuts from the oven and allow them to cool. Mix with Greek yogurt and pour into 12 protein bar containers. Leave it in a freezer for 3-4 hours before eating.

Nutritional values:

Carbohydrates 20g

Sugar 5g

Protein 11g

Total fat 12g

Sodium 45mg

Potassium 209mg

Calcium 109mg

Iron 16mg

Vitamins (Vitamin C total ascorbic acid; B-6; B-12; Folate-DFE; A-RAE; A-IU; E-alpha-tocopherol; D; D-D2+D3; K-phylloquinone; Thianin)

Calories 227

16.Fruit protein bars

Ingredients:

1 cup of mixed dried fruit

1 cup of water

1.5 cup of oatmeal

1 cup of vanilla protein powder

3 tbsp of skimmed milk

2 tsp of grated lemon peel or orange

Preparation:

Soak the dried fruit in water and let it stand for 10-15 minutes. Use electric mixer to mix the oatmeal with protein powder and milk. Spread the mixture over a baking sheet. Coat with dried fruit, sprinkle with lemon/orange peel and bake for 10 minutes at 350 degrees. Allow it to cool and cut into 5 protein bars. Put them in the fridge for 30 minutes and your protein bars are ready to eat.

Nutritional values:

Carbohydrates 41g

Sugar 23g

Protein 17g

Total fat 3g

Sodium 36mg

Potassium 213mg

Calcium 145mg

Iron 12mg

Vitamins (Vitamin C total ascorbic acid; B-6; B-12; Folate-DFE; A-RAE; A-IU; E-alpha-tocopherol; D; D-D2+D3; K-phylloquinone; Thianin)

Calories 252

17.Protein bars with cranberries and orange

Ingredients:

1 cup of grated walnuts

½ cup of walnut butter

1.5 cups of skimmed milk

1.5 cups of vanilla protein powder

1/3 cup of dried cranberries

2 tsp of grated orange peel

Preparation:

Use the ingredients to make a smooth mixture in a blender. Pour the mixture into a baking pan, greased with walnut butter. Leave it like that in the refrigerator overnight. Cut into 8 equal protein bars and keep in the fridge.

Nutritional values:

Carbohydrates 41g

Sugar 23g

Protein 17g

Total fat 3g

Sodium 23mg

Potassium 222mg

Calcium 118,4mg

Iron 31mg

Vitamins (Vitamin C total ascorbic acid; B-6; B-12; Folate-DFE; A-RAE; A-IU; E-alpha-tocopherol; D; D-D2+D3; K-phylloquinone; Thianin)

Calories 252

18. Peanut butter protein bars

Ingredients:

2 cups of oat flakes

4 scoop of protein powder

5 tablespoons of peanut butter

1/2 cup milk

Preparation:

Another super easy recipe. All you need to do is mix the ingredients in a blender and pour into protein bar containers. With this mixture, you will get 5 protein bars. Leave in the refrigerator for few hours. They are now ready to eat!

Nutritional values:

Carbohydrates 16g

Sugar 7g

Protein 16g

Total fat 2.6g

Sodium 17mg

Potassium 212mg

Calcium 105,3mg

Iron 12mg

Vitamins (Vitamin C total ascorbic acid; B-6; B-12; Folate-DFE; A-RAE; A-IU; E-alpha-tocopherol; D; D-D2+D3; K-phylloquinone; Thianin)

Calories 167

19.Almond and vanilla protein bars

Ingredients:

½ cup of barley flakes

½ cup of protein powder

2 tbsp of peanut butter

4 tbsp of grated almonds

1 glass of a lukewarm water

Preparation:

Soak the flakes into lukewarm water for about 30 minutes. Melt the peanut butter on a low temperature, in a frying pan (you can add some water if it is easier – ¼ glass should do the trick). Fry the almonds for few minutes – just to get that nice golden color. Now add the soaked flakes and protein powder. Stir well for few minutes. Remove from the heat and allow it to cool for a while. Shape 5 protein bars with this mixture and leave it in the refrigerator overnight.

Nutritional values:

Carbohydrates 23g

Sugar 16g

Protein 19g

Total fat 2,8g

Sodium 39mg

Potassium 253mg

Calcium 129,9mg

Iron 33mg

Vitamins (Vitamin C total ascorbic acid; B-6; B-12; Folate-DFE; A-RAE; A-IU; E-alpha-tocopherol; D; D-D2+D3; K-phylloquinone; Thianin)

Calories 231

20.Protein bars with dried fruit

Ingredients:

2.5 cups of oatmeal

½ cup of almonds (peeled and roasted)

½ cup of hazelnuts (peeled and roasted)

1/3 cup of honey

1 cup of dried fruit (cranberries, apricots and yellow raisins)

1 cup of sugar free apple sauce

½ teaspoon of cinnamon

Preparation:

Chop the almonds and hazelnuts into larger pieces. Dried fruits also. Use a smaller baking pan and sprinkle it with low-fat baking spray. Bake the nuts and fruits in preheated oven for about 15 minutes at 350 degrees. Remove from the oven and allow it to cool for a while. Meanwhile, mix the cinnamon, apple sauce and honey with oatmeal. You want to use a blender for this. It

should take about a minute.
Remove the nuts and fruits from the pan. Pour the mixture in it and top with the nuts. Bake for about 5 more minutes. Remove from the oven and leave it for few hours to cool. Cut into 20 protein bars and leave in the refrigerator overnight.

Nutritional values:

Carbohydrates 32,2g

Sugar 17g

Protein 19.9g

Total fat 5.6g

Sodium 31mg

Potassium 232,7mg

Calcium 126,4mg

Iron 27mg

Vitamins (Vitamin C total ascorbic acid; B-6; B-12; Folate-DFE; A-RAE; A-IU; E-alpha-tocopherol; D; D-D2+D3; K-phylloquinone; Thianin)

Calories 234

21. Amaranth Protein Bars

Ingredients:

1 cup of amaranth

3 tbsp of oats

3 tbsp of dried goji berries

3 tbsp of dried cranberries

1 tbsp of sesame

1 tbsp of sunflower seeds

2 tbsp of honey

1 large banana

1 tbsp of brown sugar

½ tsp of cinnamon

1 tbsp of oil

Preparation:

First you want to make amaranth popcorn. The procedure is the same as with regular popcorn.

Use a frying pan and sprinkle some oil on it. Put the amaranth seeds in it and fry for 10 minutes. You want to shake the frying pan several times, until the amaranth seeds are all cracked. Remove from heat and let it stand for a while.

Meanwhile, cut banana into smaller pieces. Mix with honey and other ingredients in a blender. If a mixture is too thick, the trick is to put it in a microwave for a minute. This will be enough to get a smooth mixture. Pour the mixture into baking pan, top with amaranth popcorn and bake in preheated oven for 5-10 minutes at 350 degrees. Remove from the oven, allow it to cool for a while and cut into 20 protein bars. Leave it in the refrigerator overnight.

Nutritional values:

Carbohydrates 41g

Sugar 25,1g

Protein 23,4g

Total fat 12g

Sodium 43mg

Potassium 217mg

Calcium 124,7mg

Iron 38mg

Vitamins (Vitamin C total ascorbic acid; B-6; B-12; Folate-DFE; A-RAE; A-IU; E-alpha-tocopherol; D; D-D2+D3; K-phylloquinone; Thianin)

Calories 278

22.Protein bars with sesame

Ingredients:

1.5 cup of brown sugar

1 lemon

¾ cup of sesame

Preparation:

Melt the sugar on a low temperature until you get a light brown caramel. Stir well and slowly pour the lemon juice in it. Now add sesame and mix well. Use a warm mixture to pour into protein bar containers. You should get 5 protein bars with this recipe. Allow it to cool in the refrigerator for several hours.

Nutritional values:

Carbohydrates 18g

Sugar 9g

Protein 14g

Total fat 2g

Sodium 16mg

Potassium 87mg

Calcium 8mg

Iron 7,1mg

Vitamins (Vitamin C; B-6; B-12; D; D-D2+D3;K)

Calories 112

23. Mediterranean corny with carob

Ingredients:

½ cup of oat flakes

3 tbsp of carob powder

2 tbsp of honey

1 tsp of cinnamon

pinch of salt

1 egg white, beaten in the firm snow

3 tbsp of mixed dried fruit

2 tbsp of orange juice

2 tbsp of plum jam

Preparation:

This recipe should give you 6 large protein bars. Mix well all the ingredients in a blender. Use a baking sheet and put it in a baking pan. Pour the mixture in it and bake for about 15 to 20 minutes in preheated oven at 250 degrees. Remove from heat, cut into 6 pieces and allow it to cool.

Nutritional values:

Carbohydrates 39g

Sugar 17,5g

Protein 29g

Total fat 9.4g

Sodium 39mg

Potassium 249mg

Calcium 128mg

Iron 32mg

Vitamins (Vitamin C total ascorbic acid; B-6; B-12; Folate-DFE; A-RAE; A-IU; E-alpha-tocopherol; D; D-D2+D3; K-phylloquinone; Thianin)

Calories 240

24.Sesame cubes

Ingredients:

1.5 cup of honey

1.5 cup of dark chocolate

½ cup of almond butter

1.5 cup of corn flakes

1.5 cup of sesame

1 tbsp of sesame oil

½ cup of lukewarm water

Preparation:

First you want to fry sesame seeds. Sprinkle some sesame oil on it, stir well and fry for few minutes. Seeds have to keep that light golden color. Remove from frying pan and leave it to cool.

Use a large bowl and a fork to crush corn flakes. Mix with sesame seeds, pour lukewarm water and let it stand for a while to soak the water.

Meanwhile, melt the almond butter on a low temperature. Add chocolate and honey and let it melt, stirring constantly. Remove from the heat.

Use a medium baking pen and pour the sesame seeds mixture in it. Coat with melted chocolate and cut into 8 pieces. Keep in the freezer for 2-3 hours. Remove from the freezer and keep your protein bars in the refrigerator.

Nutritional values:

Carbohydrates 41,8g

Sugar 26g

Protein 19g

Total fat 5,6g

Sodium 29mg

Potassium 249mg

Calcium 118,4mg

Iron 41mg

Vitamins (Vitamin C total ascorbic acid; B-6; B-12; Folate-DFE; A-RAE; A-IU; E-alpha-tocopherol; D; D-D2+D3; K-phylloquinone; Thianin)

Calories 239

25.Energy bars

Ingredients:

1 cup of oat flakes

4 tbsp of sunflower seeds

1/3 cup of almond flakes

2 tbsp of wheat seeds

½ cup of floral honey

3 tbsp of brown sugar

2 tbsp of peanut butter

1 tbsp of vanilla extract

pinch of salt

1 cup of chopped dried fruit (apricots, cherries, cranberries, raisins)

Preparation:

Mix the oat flakes, sunflower seeds, almond flakes and wheat seeds. Bake in preheated oven for 5-10 minutes. You can extend the baking time if you want them to be more crunchy, just don't overdo it.

Melt the sugar on a low temperature in a frying pan. Add honey, peanut butter, vanilla extract and salt. Stir well for few minutes. If the mixture is too thick, you can add some water (1/4 of a glass should do the trick). Pour the seeds in the frying pan and mix well. Divide the mixture into 10 equal pieces and coat with dried fruit. Leave in the refrigerator for few hours.

Nutritional values:

Carbohydrates 38,4g

Sugar 17,1g

Protein 27,9g

Total fat 12g

Sodium 39mg

Potassium 298mg

Calcium 112mg

Iron 29mg

Vitamins (Vitamin C total ascorbic acid; B-6; B-12; Folate-DFE; A-RAE; A-IU; E-alpha-tocopherol; D; D-D2+D3; K-phylloquinone; Thianin)

Calories 217

26.Quinoa & banana protein bars

Ingredients:

4 tbsp of quinoa

1 cup of oat flakes

1 egg

1 tbsp of honey

1 tbsp of olive oil

tsp cinnamon

pinch of salt

½ cup of raisins

1/3 cup of chopped hazelnuts

2 tbsp of sesame seeds

2 medium bananas

Preparation:

Cook quinoa for 10-15 minutes. Drain well and allow it to cool. Meanwhile mash the banana with a fork. Use a large bowl to mix oat flakes, cinnamon, egg and salt. Add the drained quinoa to the mixture.

Sprinkle olive oil in a frying pan and add hazelnuts and sesame seeds. Fry on a low temperature for 5-10 minutes. Stir well and remove from the heat.

Pour the quinoa mixture in a medium baking pan. Make the second layer with hazelnuts and sesame seeds and coat with raisins. Bake at 350 degrees for about 10 minutes. You should get a nice brown color, or check with a toothpick. Remove from the oven, cut into 10 equal pieces and allow it to cool.

Nutritional values:

Carbohydrates 38,4g

Sugar 17,1g

Protein 27,9g

Total fat 12g

Sodium 39mg

Potassium 298mg

Calcium 112mg

Iron 29mg

Vitamins (Vitamin C total ascorbic acid; B-6; B-12; Folate-DFE; A-RAE; A-IU; E-alpha-tocopherol; D; D-D2+D3; K-phylloquinone; Thianin)

Calories 150

27. Rice protein bars

Ingredients:

½ cup of sesame seeds

1.5 cup of oat flakes

1 cup of peanut butter

1.5 cup of dark chocolate (80% of cocoa)

1 cup of rice crunchies

2 cups of mixed dried fruit

½ cup of minced walnuts

1 cup of honey

Preparation:

Bake sesame seeds in preheated oven, at 350 degrees for about 10 minutes to get a nice golden color. Remove from the oven and allow it to cool. Add the oat flakes and mix well.

Mix the chocolate, peanut butter and honey and melt it in a microwave (2-3 minutes will be enough).

Now you will need a medium sized baking pan. You will make three layers – first pour the oat flakes and sesame seeds. Make another layer with melted chocolate, honey and peanut butter. Coat with rice crunchies, minced walnut and dried fruit.

Bake at 350 degrees for another 5-10 minutes. Remove from the oven and allow it to cool. Cut into 10 protein bars and leave in the refrigerator for few hours.

Nutritional values:

Carbohydrates 38,9g

Sugar 25g

Protein 23g

Total fat 6,5g

Sodium 29,3mg

Potassium 259mg

Calcium 113,7mg

Iron 29mg

Vitamins (Vitamin C total ascorbic acid; B-6; B-12; Folate-DFE; A-IU; E-alpha-tocopherol; D; D-D2+D3; K-phylloquinone; Thianin)

Calories 249

28.Coco-banana protein bars

Ingredients:

3 large bananas

6 egg whites

1 cup of coconut milk

½ cup of shredded coconut

2 tsp of vanilla extract

2 tbsp of honey

Preparation:

These protein bars are super easy to prepare. All you need is a blender. Mix the ingredients in the blender for few minutes, or until you get a smooth mixture. Pour the mixture into protein bar containers and leave in the freezer for few hours. Remove from the freezer and keep in the refrigerator.

Carbohydrates 19.8g

Sugar 4.2g

Protein 18.6g

Total fat 11.8 g

Sodium 51,5mg

Potassium 328mg

Calcium 126,8mg

Iron 29.2mg

Vitamins (Vitamin C total ascorbic acid; B-6; B-12; A-RAE; A-IU; E; D; D-D2+D3; K-phylloquinone; Thianin; Riboflavin; Niacin)

Calories 222.8 kcal

29.Chili protein bars

Ingredients:

1 cup of coconut flour

3 egg whites

1 glass of almond milk

1 tbsp of honey

1 tsp of chili

1 tbsp of cocoa

5 tbsp of grated dark chocolate (80% of cocoa)

½ glass of coconut milk

Preparation:

Place coconut flour, egg whites, almond milk, honey and chili in a food processor. Process until you get a smooth mixture. Bake the mixture in preheated oven at 350 degrees for about 10-15 minutes. Remove from the oven and cut into 5 equal protein bars.

Meanwhile boil the coconut milk and add cocoa and chocolate. Cook for 2-3 minutes and remove from heat. Allow it to cool for a while.

Now you want to soak the protein bars into the chocolate mixture. Leave them in the chocolate for 15-20 minutes. Keep your protein bars in the refrigerator.

Nutritional values:

Carbohydrates 17.8g

Sugar 5.2g

Protein 16g

Total fat 9g

Sodium 45,9mg

Potassium 342mg

Calcium 113mg

Iron 21.2mg

Vitamins (Vitamin C; B-6; B-12; A-RAE; D; D-D2+D3; K-phylloquinone; Thianin; Riboflavin; Niacin)

Calories 234 kcal

30.Greek yogurt protein bars

Ingredients:

1 cup of Greek yogurt

1 large banana

3 egg whites

½ cup of minced walnuts

1 tsp of vanilla extract

½ cup of coconut flour

1 tbsp of brown sugar

½ cup of cranberries

½ cup of minced hazelnuts

Preparation:

Mix the Greek yogurt with banana, egg whites, minced walnuts and vanilla in a food processor. You want to make a smooth mixture. Leave that mixture in the refrigerator for at least an hour. Remove from the refrigerator, make 8 protein bars. Coat them with cranberries, brown sugar and hazelnuts and roll into coconut flour. Bake on a baking sheet, in preheated oven at 350 degrees for 10 minutes. Remove from the oven and allow it to cool. Keep them in the refrigerator.

Nutritional values:

Carbohydrates 21.9g

Sugar 9.7g

Protein 19.5g

Total fat 15g

Sodium 46,3mg

Potassium 312mg

Calcium 148mg

Iron 30mg

Vitamins (Vitamin C; B-6; B-12; A-RAE; D; D-D2+D3; K-phylloquinone; Thianin; Riboflavin; Niacin)

Calories 216 kcal

31.Apple juice protein bars

Ingredients:

1 cup of oatmeal

½ cup of flour

¼ cup of chopped almonds and hazelnuts

¼ cup of raisins

¼ cup of freshly squeezed apple juice

¼ cup of honey

½ tsp of cinnamon

2 tbsp of oil

1 tbsp of melted almond butter

Preparation:

Mix all the dry ingredients. Add oil, almond butter, apple juice and honey. Stir well to get a smooth mixture. Pour the mixture on a baking sheet. It should be about 0.5 inch thick. Bake in preheated oven at 250 degrees for 15-20 minutes. Remove from the oven, cut into 10 protein bars and let it stand in the refrigerator for few hours.

Nutritional values:

Carbohydrates 21g

Sugar 6g

Protein 19,3g

Total fat 12g

Sodium 49,5mg

Potassium 318mg

Calcium 112mg

Iron 23.2mg

Vitamins (Vitamin C; B-6; B-12; A-RAE; D; D-D2+D3; K-phylloquinone; Thianin; Riboflavin; Niacin)

Calories 212 kcal

32. Protein bars with figs

Ingredients:

1 cup of chopped almonds

¼ cup of chopped dried figs

¼ cup of chopped dried plums

¼ cup of raisins

2 tsp of cinnamon

2 tbsp of oat flakes

½ cup of almond milk

Preparation:

Mix the almonds, dried figs, plums, raisins, cinnamon and oat flakes in a food processor. Add milk and mix for another 1-2 minutes. Place this mixture on a baking sheet and bake in preheated oven at 225 degrees for about 45 minutes. The mixture must be very dry. Remove from the oven, cut into 10 protein bars and keep in a dry and cold place.

If it is easier for you, you can make protein bars before baking/drying. Use protein bars mold and shape the mixture with it.

Little secret: All those who have a dehydrator, use it for this recipe. It will preserve all the nutrients.

Nutritional values:

Carbohydrates 20g

Sugar 7,6g

Protein 19g

Total fat 12g

Sodium 58mg

Potassium 312mg

Calcium 140,2mg

Iron 23mg

Vitamins (Vitamin C; B-6; B-12; A-RAE; D; D-D2+D3; K-phylloquinone; Thianin; Riboflavin; Niacin)

Calories 219 kcal

33.Power mix protein bars

Ingredients:

2 large oranges

1 tbsp of light honey

3 tbsp of brown sugar

6 tbsp of almond butter

8 tbsp of maple syrup

2 tbsp of cranberries jam

3 tbsp of hazelnuts

3 tbsp of white almonds

2 tbsp of walnuts

2 tbsp of cracked amaranth

3 tbsp of golden raisins

10 tbsp of fine oat flakes

8 tbsp of grated dark chocolate (80% of cocoa)

Preparation:

Wash and dry the oranges. Finely peel the scrub. Squeeze the juice from the oranges, add sugar and honey and boil on a high temperature with constant stirring, until all the liquid evaporates. You will get a very thick jam.

Cut hazelnuts, almonds and walnuts into small pieces.

Mix the almond butter, maple syrup and cranberries jam by using an electric mixer. Put it in a microwave for 1-2 minutes. Remove from the microwave and mix with orange jam, nuts, amaranth and oats. You will get a very thick mixture. Keep it like that. Now you will need protein bar molds. Shape 10 protein bars and bake them in preheated oven for 10 minutes at 350 degrees. Remove from the oven and allow it to cool.

Melt the chocolate in the microwave for few minutes. Soak your protein bars into the chocolate and leave in the refrigerator for several hours.

Nutritional values:

Carbohydrates 28g

Sugar 11g

Protein 23g

Total fat 17.8 g

Sodium 58,3g

Potassium 369mg

Calcium 141mg

Iron 34mg

Vitamins (Vitamin C; B-6; B-12; A-RAE; D; D-D2+D3; K-phylloquinone; Thianin; Riboflavin; Niacin)

Calories 268.8 kcal

34.Apricot protein bars

Ingredients:

4 tbsp of brown sugar

3 tbsp of honey

4 tbsp of peanut butter

2 tbsp of freshly squeezed apricot juice

1 tbsp of grated orange zest

1 cup of rice flakes

½ cup of chopped apricots

½ cup of chopped walnuts

Preparation:

Combine all the ingredients in a large bowl. Use an electric mixer to get a homogeneous mass. Preheat the oven to 250 degrees. Pour the mixture on a baking sheet and bake for about 15 minutes. It should get golden brown color. Remove from the oven, cut into 5 protein bars and keep in a dry and cold place.

Nutritional values:

Carbohydrates 20.7g

Sugar 7.4g

Protein 19.5g

Total fat 13g

Sodium 49mg

Potassium 294mg

Calcium 112,8mg

Iron 27mg

Vitamins (Vitamin C; B-6; B-12; A-RAE; D; D-D2+D3; K-phylloquinone; Thianin; Riboflavin; Niacin)

Calories 259 kcal

35.Protein bars with mixed fruits

Ingredients:

¼ cup of chopped dried figs

¼ cup of chopped dates

¼ cup of sliced prunes

¼ cup of white raisins

¼ cup of chopped dried orange

¼ cup of chopped dried plums

1 glass of fresh orange juice

1 glass of fresh lemon juice

¼ cup of ground walnuts

¼ cup of ground hazelnuts

¼ cup of honey

a few drops of rum extract

¼ cup of chopped pineapple

1 cup of melted dark chocolate (80% of cocoa)

¼ cup of cocoa

¼ cup of almond butter

Preparation:

Mix well fruits, nuts, honey, orange and lemon juice in a large bowl. Keep the mixture in a bowl. Melt the almond butter on a low temperature, add rum extract, dark chocolate and cocoa. Keep cooking until the boiling point. Stir constantly! Remove from the heat and use this mixture to bind the fruit and nuts mixture. Mix well and shape 18 protein bars. Keep them in the refrigerator for several hours. These protein bars are very delicious and crunchy.

Nutritional values:

Carbohydrates 27g

Sugar 9g

Protein 23.8g

Total fat 17.8 g

Sodium 64mg

Potassium 417mg

Calcium 139mg

Iron 31mg

Vitamins (Vitamin C; B-6; B-12; A-RAE; D; D-D2+D3; K-phylloquinone; Thianin; Riboflavin; Niacin)

Calories 289kcal

36. Crispy protein bars

Ingredients:

½ cup of dried figs

¼ cup of dried coconut

¼ cup of roasted peanuts

¼ cup of wheat flakes

¼ cup of rice flakes

3 tbsp of roasted wheat

½ cup of honey

½ cup of peanut butter

3 tbsp of agave syrup

4 tbsp of brown sugar

¼ tsp of ground cinnamon

1 tsp of vanilla extract

Preparation:

Combine figs, dried coconut and roasted peanut in a large bowl. Add wheat, roasted wheat, rice and stir well.

In a smaller bowl, bind honey with peanut butter, agave syrup and brown sugar. Cook for several minutes on a low temperature until the brown sugar is fully dissolved. Add cinnamon, vanilla extract and bring it to the boiling point. Remove from the heat. Pour this mixture over the prepared nuts and fruits and mix well.

Use a medium sized baking sheet, put the mixture in it and bake for about 20 minutes at 225 degrees. Remove from the oven, cut into 24 protein bars and leave them in the refrigerator for at least few hours.

Nutritional values:

Carbohydrates 29g

Sugar 11,3g

Protein 26g

Total fat 11g

Sodium 61,1mg

Potassium 287mg

Calcium 134mg

Iron 31mg

Vitamins (Vitamin C; B-6; B-12; A-RAE; D; D-D2+D3; K-phylloquinone; Thianin; Riboflavin; Niacin)

Calories 254 kcal

37.Cottage cheese & blueberries protein bars

Ingredients:

1 cup of low fat cottage cheese

1 cup of Greek yogurt

2 egg whites

½ cup of blueberries

4 tbsp of brown sugar

1 tsp of vanilla extract

½ cup of coconut flour

Preparation:

Put all the ingredients, except coconut flour, into the food processor. Mix well to get a smooth mixture. Use protein bar mold to create 10 equal protein bars. Sprinkle them with coconut flour and freeze for few hours. Remove from the freezer and keep in the refrigerator.

Nutritional values:

Carbohydrates 18.7g

Sugar 5.2g

Protein 16.7g

Total fat 16.5 g

Sodium 54,7mg

Potassium 339mg

Calcium 138,5mg

Iron 24.8mg

Vitamins (Vitamin C; B-6; B-12; A-RAE; D; D-D2+D3; K-phylloquinone; Thianin; Riboflavin; Niacin)

Calories 236.7 kcal

38.Chia seeds protein bars

Ingredients:

1 cup of minced chia seeds

½ cup of walnuts

½ cup of hazelnuts

½ cup of cranberries

1 cup of low fat cheese

½ cup of honey

1 tbsp of vanilla extract

1 tsp of cinnamon

1 scoop of protein powder

low fat baking spray

Preparation:

Mix the chia seeds with nuts and cheese. Use protein bar molds to make 8 equal protein bars.

With an electric mixer, combine honey, cinnamon, vanilla extract and protein powder. Now you have to pour this mixture over the protein bars.

Preheat the oven at 350 degrees. Sprinkle the baking sheet with low fat baking spray and bake protein bars for about 20 minutes, until you get a light brown color. Remove from the oven and allow it to cool. Keep in the refrigerator for several hours.

Nutritional values:

Carbohydrates 14.9g

Sugar 5.3g

Protein 18.3g

Total fat 14.6 g

Sodium 52,7mg

Potassium 326mg

Calcium 127,3mg

Iron 26.3mg

Vitamins (Vitamin C; B-6; B-12; A-RAE; D; D-D2+D3; K-phylloquinone; Thianin; Riboflavin; Niacin)

Calories 226.3 kcal

39.Oatmeal protein bars

Ingredients:

1 cup of oatmeal

¼ cup of cornflakes

½ cup of crushed hazelnuts

6 - 8 pieces of prunes cut into cubes

1/3 cup of raisins

1/3 cup of sesame seeds

1/3 cup of flaxseed

½ cup of brown sugar

½ cup of grated chocolate (80% of cocoa)

1 medium sized orange

1 tsp of cinnamon

1 tsp of rum extract

½ cup of peanut butter

2 tbsp of honey

¼ cup of grated chocolate (80% of cocoa) – for decoration

Preparation:

Combine all dry ingredients in a large bowl. Wash the orange, grate the peel and squeeze it. Use a frying pan to melt the peanut butter on a low temperature. Add sugar, rum extract, cinnamon, rind and orange juice. Stir well and let it cook for 3-5 minutes. Then add the dry ingredients into the frying pan and stir well again. Add honey. Remove from the heat, allow it to cool for a while and make 15 equal protein bars. Decorate with some more chocolate and keep in the refrigerator overnight.

Nutritional values:

Carbohydrates 27.2g

Sugar 9.2g

Protein 26.3g

Total fat 12.8 g

Sodium 96,5mg

Potassium 356mg

Calcium 124,8mg

Iron 29.2mg

Vitamins (Vitamin C; B-6; B-12; A-RAE; D; D-D2+D3; K-phylloquinone; Thianin; Riboflavin; Niacin)

Calories 278.3 kcal

40.Honey protein bars

Ingredients:

½ cup of almond butter

½ cup of honey

2 eggs

1/3 cup of ground almonds

½ cup of dried apricots – cut into small pieces

¼ cup of roasted hazelnuts, finely chopped

¼ cup of dried cherries, finely chopped

¼ cup of sesame

1/3 cup of oats

1 tbsp of sesame oil

Preparation:

For this recipe, you will need a small baking sheet. Sprinkle some sesame oil over it.

Whisk the almond butter with honey until creamy mixture, then add the beaten eggs, nuts and fruits. Continue to whisk this mixture for few more minutes.

Preheat the oven at 350 degrees. Pour the mixture on a baking sheet and bake for about 20-25 minutes, until golden color. Remove from the oven and cool for about 10 minutes. Cut into 10 equal protein bars. You can add some more honey on top, but this is optional and increases the nutritional value. The good thing about these protein bars is that they are perfect warm as well as cold.

Nutritional values:

Carbohydrates 28.7g

Sugar 9.2g

Protein 27.5g

Total fat 14.8 g

Sodium 51,5mg

Potassium 328mg

Calcium 126,8mg

Iron 29.2mg

Vitamins (Vitamin C; B-6; B-12; A-RAE; D; D-D2+D3; K-phylloquinone; Thianin; Riboflavin; Niacin)

Calories 248.8 kcal

41.Protein bars with oatmeal and raisins

Ingredients:

½ cup of oat flakes

½ cup of chopped walnuts

½ cup of raisins

½ cup of chopped dry plums

½ cup of sunflower seeds

½ cup of melted coconut oil

¼ cup of chia seeds

¼ cup of honey

¼ cup of chocolate (70% of cocoa)

1 tsp of cinnamon

Preparation:

Preheat the oven at 350 degrees. Use a saucepan to melt the chocolate and coconut oil on a very low temperature. Stir well. Mix it with other ingredients in a large bowl. Spread the mixture on a baking sheet and bake for 15 minutes. Allow it to cool and keep in the refrigerator for few hours.

Nutritional values:

Carbohydrates 27.6g

Sugar 9.2g

Protein 25.3g

Total fat 15.8 g

Sodium 61,2mg

Potassium 229mg

Calcium 134,4mg

Iron 24.3mg

Vitamins (Vitamin C; B-6; B-12; A-RAE; D; D-D2+D3; K-phylloquinone; Thianin; Riboflavin; Niacin)

Calories 228 kcal

42.Protein bars with dates

Ingredients:

½ cup of chopped dates

¼ cup of chopped dried apricots

¼ cup of raisins

¼ cup of dried cranberries

1 tbsp of peanut butter

¼ tsp of ground cinnamon

5 tbsp of agave syrup

¼ cup of grated walnuts

¼ cup of grated almonds

Preparation:

Use an electric food processor to process dates, apricots, raisins and cranberries. Add the peanut butter, cinnamon, agave syrup and mix well. Pour this mixture on a baking sheet. Spread the walnuts and almonds on top of it and press a little bit with your hands. Cover with adhesive foil and place in the refrigerator for at least 3-4 hours. Cut into 10 equal protein bars.

Nutritional values:

Carbohydrates 23.4g

Sugar 5.2g

Protein 19.5g

Total fat 13.4 g

Sodium 41,4mg

Potassium 353mg

Calcium 135,5mg

Iron 19mg

Vitamins (Vitamin C; B-6; B-12; A-RAE; D; D-D2+D3; K-phylloquinone; Thianin; Riboflavin; Niacin)

Calories 236.6 kcal

43.Protein bars with pistachios

Ingredients:

1 cup of roasted pistachios – chopped into small pieces

1 cup of chopped dates

1 tsp of cocoa

1 tsp of cinnamon

2 tsp of vanilla sugar

1 lemon

pinch of salt

1 cup of mixed chopped dried fruit

Preparation:

Use an electric blender to mix dates and pistachios. Add other ingredients and mix for another few minutes. Use this mixture to create 10 protein bars. You can do it manually or you can use protein bar molds. Leave it in the refrigerator overnight.

Nutritional values:

Carbohydrates 19.7g

Sugar 7.4g

Protein 18.5g

Total fat 13.5 g

Sodium 31,8mg

Potassium 326mg

Calcium 124mg

Iron 23.2mg

Vitamins (Vitamin C; B-6; B-12; A-RAE; D; D-D2+D3; K-phylloquinone; Thianin; Riboflavin; Niacin)

Calories 243.7 kcal

44.Protein bars molasses

Ingredients:

½ cup of dark sugar syrup - molasses

¼ cup of peanut butter

½ cup of brown sugar

¼ cup of walnuts

¼ cup of chopped dried apricots

¼ cup of chopped dried figs

1 cup of oat flakes

¼ cup of pumpkin seeds

Preparation:

Preheat the oven at 350 degrees. Chop the walnuts into very small pieces. Use a saucepan to mix the peanut butter, sugar and sugar syrup. Cook it for about 5 minutes on a very low temperature. Stir well. Let it boil. The mixture should be moist and slightly sticky, not dry.

Remove from the heat and mix with the walnuts, dried fruits, oat flakes and pumpkin seeds.

Bake for about 30 minutes. Allow it to cool for about an hour or even two before you cut it into 10 equal protein bars.

Nutritional values:

Carbohydrates 26.4g

Sugar 4.6g

Protein 19.5g

Total fat 12.2 g

Sodium 21,9mg

Potassium 368mg

Calcium 111mg

Iron 25.3mg

Vitamins (Vitamin C; B-6; B-12; A-RAE; D; D-D2+D3; K-phylloquinone; Thianin; Riboflavin; Niacin)

Calories 219 kcal

45. Protein bars with turmeric and raspberries

Ingredients:

½ cup of soy milk

1 cup of smashed banana

1 cup of coconut flour

½ cup of turmeric

2 egg whites

½ cup of grated walnuts

½ cup of raspberries

Preparation:

This recipe is very easy to prepare. It does not need any cooking or baking. All you need is a blender to mix all the ingredients for few minutes. Pour the mixture into protein bar molds and leave in the freezer for few hours. When finished, keep them in the refrigerator.

Nutritional values:

Carbohydrates 21.3g

Sugar 6.4g

Protein 19.5g

Total fat 11.4 g

Sodium 33,7mg

Potassium 343mg

Calcium 133mg

Iron 13.2mg

Vitamins (Vitamin C; B-6; B-12; A-RAE; D; D-D2+D3; K-phylloquinone; Thianin; Riboflavin; Niacin)

Calories 232.4 kcal

46.Protein bars with red pepper

Ingredients:

3 tbsp of cocoa powder

1.5 cup of almonds

½ cup of buckwheat flour

2 tsp of cinnamon

½ tsp of ground red pepper

½ cup of chopped chocolate (80% of cocoa)

1 cup of brown sugar

1 cup of honey

Preparation:

Preheat oven to 250 degrees. Mix the cocoa, chopped almonds, buckwheat flour, cinnamon and pepper in a large bowl. Use a saucepan to melt the chocolate, sugar and honey on a low temperature. Stir well and add the dry mixture to it. Mix well and remove from the heat. Allow it to cool for a while and make 10 protein bars with your hands or with the mold. Sprinkle them with some more cocoa powder, just for decoration. Bake for about 30 minutes. Remove from the oven, allow it to cool and keep in the refrigerator.

Nutritional values:

Carbohydrates 21g

Sugar 5.4g

Protein 19.3g

Total fat 12.3 g

Sodium 32,2mg

Potassium 236mg

Calcium 121mg

Iron 23,2mg

Vitamins (Vitamin C; B-6; B-12; A-RAE; D; D-D2+D3; K-phylloquinone; Thianin; Riboflavin; Niacin)

Calories 219 kcal

47.Protein bars with blackberries

Ingredients:

1 cup of blackberries

1 cup of cornflakes

1 cup of low fat cheese

1 tsp of blackberries extract

½ cup of rice flour

Preparation:

Another super easy recipe. Mix the ingredients with an electric mixer. Use protein bar molds to create 10 protein bars with this mixture. Preheat oven to 350 degrees and bake your protein bars for 15 minutes. Remove from the oven, allow it to cool for about an hour before you put it into the refrigerator.

Nutritional values:

Carbohydrates 19,1g

Sugar 3.4g

Protein 18.5g

Total fat 13.2 g

Sodium 35,2mg

Potassium 392mg

Calcium 121mg

Iron 21.3mg

Vitamins (Vitamin C; B-6; B-12; A-RAE; D; D-D2+D3; K-phylloquinone; Thianin; Riboflavin; Niacin)

Calories 211 kcal

48.Toffee protein bars

Ingredients:

½ cup of almond butter

½ cup of brown sugar

2 tbsp of maple syrup

1.5 cup of oat flakes

pinch of salt

Preparation:

Melt the almond butter and sugar on a low temperature. It should not boil, but it must have golden brown color. Add maple syrup and mix well for another minute. Remove from the heat, add salt and oat flakes. It will be a very sticky mixture.

Pour that mixture on a baking sheet and bake in preheated at 225 degrees, for 20-25 minutes. Remove from the oven, allow it to cool for about an hour, and cut into 6 equal protein bars. It is very important for the mixture to cool completely.

Otherwise you will not be able to cut it properly. Keep them in the refrigerator.

Nutritional values:

Carbohydrates 21.7g

Sugar 5.4g

Protein 13.5g

Total fat 14.2 g

Sodium 32,4mg

Potassium 311mg

Calcium 133mg

Iron 21.4mg

Vitamins (Vitamin C; B-6; B-12; A-RAE; D; D-D2+D3; K-phylloquinone; Thianin; Riboflavin; Niacin)

Calories 212 kcal

Made in the USA
Las Vegas, NV
29 December 2021

39766492R00098